T0345863

Math and Max

Brian Sargent

Illustrated by Dominic Bugatto

OXFORD
UNIVERSITY PRESS

198 Madison Avenue
New York, NY 10016 USA

Great Clarendon Street, Oxford OX2 6DP UK

Oxford University Press is a department of the University of Oxford. It furthers the University's objective of excellence in research, scholarship, and education by publishing worldwide in

Oxford   New York
Auckland Cape Town Dar es Salaam
Hong Kong Karachi Kuala Lumpur Madrid
Melbourne Mexico City Nairobi New Delhi
Shanghai Taipei Toronto

With offices in
Argentina Austria Brazil Chile Czech Republic
France Greece Guatemala Hungary Italy Japan
Poland Portugal Singapore South Korea
Switzerland Thailand Turkey Ukraine Vietnam

OXFORD and OXFORD ENGLISH are registered trademarks of Oxford University Press.

Photocopying

Any websites referred to in this publication are in the public domain and their addresses are provided by Oxford University Press for information only. Oxford University Press disclaims any responsibility for the content.

Executive Publishing Manager: Stephanie Karras
Managing Editor: Sharon Sargent
Design Manager: Stacy Merlin
Project Coordinator: Sarah Dentry
Production Layout Artist: Colleen Ho
Cover Design: Colleen Ho, Stacy Merlin, Michael Steinhofer
Manufacturing Manager: Shanta Persaud
Manufacturing Controller: Eve Wong

ISBN: 978 0 19474034 0 (BOOK)

ISBN: 978 0 19474039 5 (OPD READING LIBRARY)

ISBN: 978 0 19474056 2 (WORKPLACE READING LIBRARY)

Printed in China

10 9 8 7 6 5 4 3

This book is printed on paper from certified and well-managed sources.

Many thanks to Pronk&Associates, Kelly Stern, and Meg Brooks for a job well done.

Math and Max

Table of Contents

A. Match the pictures with the words.

a.
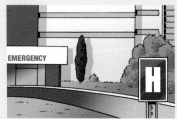

b.

c.

d.

e.

f.
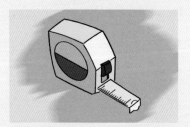

g.

h.

_e_ 1. algebra   ___ 4. draw   ___ 7. painter

___ 2. artist   ___ 5. engineer   ___ 8. tape measure

___ 3. calculator   ___ 6. hospital

B. Answer the questions.

1. What types of math can you name?
2. How do you use math in your life?
3. What is a job that uses math?
4. Do you use math in your job?
5. Why is knowing math an important job skill?

C. Read the chapter titles of this book. Look at the pictures in the book. Then guess the answers to the questions. Circle *a* or *b*.

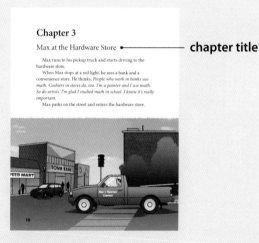

chapter title

1. What is Max's job?
   a. He's a painter.
   b. He's a doctor.

2. Where is Max working?
   a. He's working at an office building.
   b. He's working at a hospital.

3. Who does Max meet in Chapter 4?
   a. He meets an artist.
   b. He meets an engineer.

Chapter 1

Many Rooms to Paint

Max is a painter. He paints the inside of buildings. He likes working in big buildings. Big buildings have a lot of rooms, and that means more money for Max.

Today is the first day of Max's new job. He's going to paint some rooms in a new hospital. Max wants to know how much money he's going to make. He uses algebra to find out. Algebra uses equations to answer math questions.

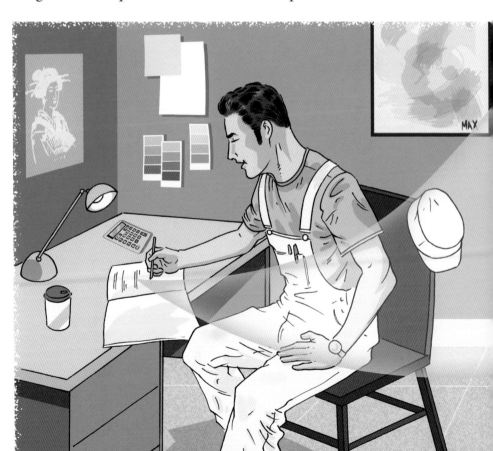

Max makes $150 for each room he paints. The number of rooms he's going to paint is x. The total amount of money he's going to make is y. He writes an equation: $150x = y$.

Max is going to paint 20 rooms, so x equals 20. Max uses his calculator. For 20 rooms, he's going to make $3,000.

The pay is nice, he thinks, *but 20 rooms is a lot of work. I need to start early.*

Max arrives on the job at 7 a.m. He brings his paintbrushes and rollers. He also brings a tape measure and a calculator. Painting is hard work. Math makes Max's job easier. It helps him find answers. Now Max needs to know how much paint to buy. He uses geometry to find out how much paint he needs. Geometry is a kind of math that measures shapes and areas.

Each wall has a length and a height. *I multiply the length by the height. That gives me the area*, Max thinks.

Each room has two long walls and two short walls. Max measures the walls in one room. Then he uses his calculator. The room has 320 square feet of wall area. Max checks the other rooms. They're the same. Now Max can calculate how much paint to buy.

HEIGHT

LENGTH

HEIGHT X LENGTH = AREA

Reading Check

A. Mark the sentences T (true) or F (false).

_F_ 1. Max doesn't like to paint large buildings.

____ 2. Max makes $320 for each room he paints.

____ 3. Math helps Max find the area of the walls.

____ 4. Max is going to guess how much paint he needs.

B. Choose *a* or *b*.

1. ____ helps Max find out how much money he's going to make.
   (a.) Algebra
   b. Hospital

2. It's easy to multiply or divide large numbers using a ____ .
   a. painter
   b. calculator

3. Max uses ____ to find the area of the walls.
   a. geometry
   b. rollers

4. Max uses his ____ to find the height and length of the room.
   a. equation
   b. tape measure

C. Complete the summary. Use the words in the box.

algebra	calculate	geometry
hospital	math	~~painter~~

This chapter is about a ____painter____ named Max.
He's painting rooms in a _____ . Max uses two
kinds of _____ in his work. _____
helps him find out how much money he's going to make. With
_____ , he finds the wall area of each room. The
area helps him _____ how much paint to buy.

**What's going to happen next? What do you think?
Circle your guess, _yes_ or _no_.**

1. Is Max going to meet
   an artist?

   yes   no

2. Is Max going to measure
   a flagpole?

   yes   no

3. Is the artist going to buy
   paint with Max?

   yes   no

Chapter 2

Lana and the Flagpole

Max leaves the building to buy paint. He meets Lana. She's a famous artist. She likes to draw and paint, but her favorite kind of art is sculpture. Lana likes to make big sculptures.

Lana is going to make a new sculpture for the hospital. Today she's looking at the location for the sculpture. It's near the hospital entrance. Lana is thinking about her sculpture. How big can she make it?

There's a tall flagpole in front of the hospital. Lana's new sculpture can't be taller than the flagpole.

"How tall is that flagpole?" Lana asks.

Max says, "I don't know, but I have a tape measure." Max offers his tape measure to Lana.

"Thanks, but I can't use that," Lana says. "The flagpole is too tall. And I know how to measure it without a tape measure. Watch this!"

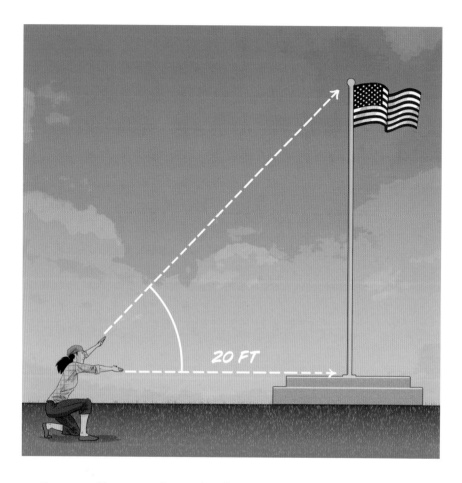

20 FT

Lana walks away from the flagpole. Then she says, "Please measure the distance between me and the pole."

Max measures 20 feet. Lana points to the top of the flagpole with one hand. Then she points to the bottom with her other hand. The space between Lana's arms makes an angle. She says, "I can use this angle to calculate the height of the flagpole."

"How?" asks Max.

"I use trigonometry," answers Lana. "Trigonometry is a kind of math. It uses angles. We know the distance to the flagpole. It's 20 feet. Now, I need to measure the angle with a special tool," says Lana. "Let me show you."

"No, thanks," says Max. "I'm too busy today. There are a lot of rooms to paint in this hospital. I need to buy paint and start working."

Reading Check

A. Circle the correct answer.

1. What happens to Max in this chapter?
   a. He buys paint.
   b. He meets Lana.
   c. He arrives at work.

2. What is Lana's problem?
   a. She can't draw a picture of the flagpole.
   b. She's too busy to talk.
   c. She needs to measure the flagpole.

3. What does Lana do?
   a. She uses trigonometry.
   b. She uses a tape measure.
   c. She goes home.

4. Why does Max leave Lana?
   a. It's time for lunch.
   b. He needs to buy paint.
   c. He doesn't like math.

B. Match the pictures with the words.

 d 1. draw   ___ 3. artist   ___ 5. top
 ___ 2. sculpture   ___ 4. angle   ___ 6. bottom

C. Circle the best summary for each page.

1. What happens on page 10?

    a. Max meets Lana.
    b. Lana likes to draw and paint.
    c. Max talks about Lana's sculpture.

2. What happens on page 12?

    a. Lana stops and turns around.
    b. Lana shows Max how to measure the height of the flagpole.
    c. Max measures the flagpole.

What's Next in Chapter 3?

What's going to happen next? What do you think? Circle your guess, *yes* or *no*.

1. Is Max going to walk to the hardware store?

    yes   no

2. Is Max going to see Lana at the hardware store?

    yes   no

3. Is Max going to wait in line to buy paint?

    yes   no

Chapter 3

Max at the Hardware Store

Max runs to his pickup truck and starts driving to the hardware store.

When Max stops at a red light, he sees a bank and a convenience store. He thinks, *People who work in banks use math. Cashiers in stores do, too. I'm a painter and I use math. So do artists. I'm glad I studied math in school. I know it's really important.*

Max parks on the street and enters the hardware store.

Max looks in his notebook. Each room has 320 square feet of wall. Max needs to paint 20 rooms. He uses his calculator and multiplies 320 by 20. The answer is 6,400. Max needs to paint 6,400 square feet.

Max reads the label on a paint can. One gallon paints about 400 square feet. Max uses his calculator and divides 6,400 by 400. The answer is 16. Max needs to buy 16 cans of paint.

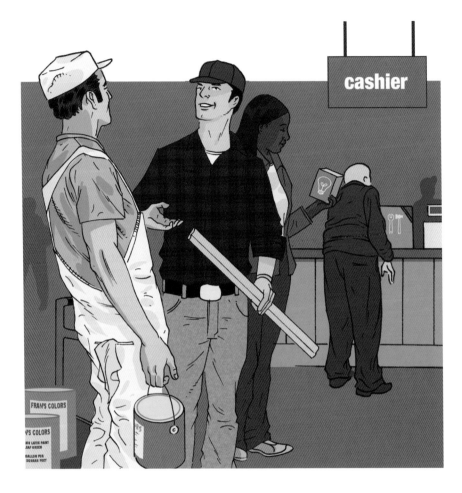

The hardware store is busy. Max waits in the checkout line to buy his paint. Another man standing in line says, "This is taking a long time."

Max says, "Yes, it is. I have to get back to the hospital. I have a big painting job there."

The man says, "I'm working at the hospital, too! My name's Joe."

"Hi, Joe. I'm Max," Max says. "What do you do?"

Joe says, "I'm a carpenter. I'm installing doors today."

Max says, "Another job that uses math!"

Joe says, "Yes, carpenters use math all the time on the job. You know what we say: 'Measure twice, cut once!'"

Now the line is moving. "You're next," Max tells Joe.

Joe pays the cashier. Then Max buys his paint.

Outside, Joe says, "The next time we need supplies, let's drive here together. That can save us money. I don't need a calculator to know that!"

A. Mark the sentences T (true) or F (false). Change the false sentences. Make them true.

_F_ 1. Max goes to a convenience store to buy paint.

   Max goes to a hardware store to buy paint.

___ 2. Max thinks only painters use math in their jobs.

___ 3. Joe is installing windows in the hospital.

___ 4. Max thinks math is important.

B. Label the pictures. Use the words in the box.

carpenter	cashier	~~checkout line~~
gallon of paint	hardware store	supplies

1.

checkout line

2.

_____

3.

_____

4.

FRAN'S COLORS

INTERIOR LATEX PAINT
LEAF GREEN

1 GALLON FOR
400 SQUARE FEET

_____

5.

POWER TOOLS

_____

6.

_____

C. Circle the best summary of each page.

1. What happens on page 16?
    a. Max stops at a red light.
    b. Max drives to the hardware store in his truck.
    c. Max pays the cashier.

2. What happens on page 17?
    a. Max looks in his notebook.
    b. Max reads the label on a paint can.
    c. Max calculates how much paint he needs.

3. What happens on page 18?
    a. The hardware store is busy.
    b. Max meets a carpenter as he waits in line.
    c. The carpenter's name is Joe.

What's Next in Chapter 4?

What's going to happen next? What do you think? Circle or write your guess.

What is Max going to do?
    a. He's going to drive to another store for more supplies.
    b. He's going to paint the rooms in the hospital.
    c. He's going to install doors with the carpenter.
    d. other: _____

Chapter 4

Max and the Engineer

Max returns to the hospital. He carries two cans of paint into an empty room. Max opens one can and starts painting.

As Max finishes one wall, a man walks into the room. The man is wearing a hard hat and carrying the plans for the hospital. He looks around the room. He looks at his plans. Then he sees Max.

"Hi. I'm David," says the man. "I'm one of the engineers. I'm checking the building."

"What exactly are you checking?" asks Max.

"I'm checking that the workers followed my plans. I want to make sure that the building is safe."

"What do you mean?" Max asks.

David thinks for a minute and then says, "Well, a building has beams, right? Engineers choose beams that make the building strong and safe."

"How do you choose?" asks Max. "Let me guess. You use math!"

"That's right. I use calculus, which is a kind of math," David says.

"The beams are strong, but too much weight can make a beam break. Calculus tells me how much weight is okay," says David.

"How does it do that?" Max asks.

"I use one mathematical equation for the beam. Then I use another for the weight of the building," David explains.

"Equations! I use equations in my work, too," Max says.

David says, "Really? Then let me show you this."

David takes Max's paintbrush and draws an equation on the wall. "This is how calculus works," he says. "This shows—"

Max holds out his hand and says, "Excuse me, David. Calculus is your job, but painting is my job. I'm sorry, but I need to get back to work."

David laughs and returns the paintbrush to Max.

"You have a lot of rooms to paint," says David. "Do you have any help?"

"Yes," Max says. "Math helps me!"

A. Circle the correct answer.

1. Who does Max meet inside the hospital?
   a. Joe
   b. David
   c. Lana

2. Why is David at the hospital?
   a. He wants to paint some walls.
   b. He's meeting Max for lunch.
   c. He's checking the building.

3. What does Max learn from David?
   a. Engineers design safe buildings.
   b. Engineers like to paint.
   c. Engineers wear hard hats.

4. Who uses math on the job?
   a. Max
   b. David
   c. Max and David

B. Look at the picture. Complete the words.

1. ca __l__ cul __u__ s
2. pl ____ ns
3. ____ ng ____ nee ____
4. bea ____
5. b ____ ild ____ ng

C. Match the chapter with the correct summary.

_C_ 1. Chapter 1

     2. Chapter 2

     3. Chapter 3

     4. Chapter 4

a. Max meets David, an engineer. David is checking that the building is safe. Max learns that engineers use calculus in their job.

b. Max meets Lana, an artist. Lana is planning a sculpture for the hospital. Lana uses trigonometry to find the height for her sculpture.

c. Max, a painter, gets a job painting rooms in a hospital. It's going to be a lot of work. He uses math to help him with his job.

d. Max goes to the hardware store to buy paint. He meets a carpenter in the checkout line. The carpenter is also working at the hospital.

What's Next?

Think about what Max is going to do now. Write 2 or 3 sentences.

A. Read a help-wanted ad.

- What is the job in this help-wanted ad?
- How does a person in this job use math?

CASHIER NEEDED

Food and More Store

part-time, 10+ hours/week
some weekend work
$8/hr

Phone 555-1774

B. Work with a partner. Make your own help-wanted ad.

- Make a help-wanted ad for a job that uses math.
- Discuss how people use math in this job.
- Show your help-wanted ad to the class. Tell how a person uses math in this job.

Useful Expressions

This job is _____ [say the name of the job].

This job is at _____ [say the name of a business].

A person needs to (add / subtract / multiply / divide) in this job.

Shared vocabulary from the *OPD* and *Math and Max*

x = the sale price
$x = 79.00 - .40\,(79.00)$
$x = \$47.40$

algebra
[al′jə brə]

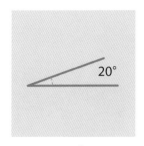

20°

angle
[ăng′gəl]

artist
[är′tĭst]

beam
[bēm]

building
[bĭl′dĭng]

calculator
[kăl′kyə lā′tər]

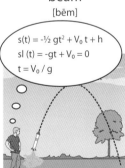

$s(t) = -\tfrac{1}{2}\,gt^2 + V_0\,t + h$
$sl\,(t) = -gt + V_0 = 0$
$t = V_0 / g$

calculus
[kăl′kyə ləs]

carpenter
[kär′pən tər]

cashier
[kă shïr′]

draw
[drö]

engineer
[ĕn/jə nïr/]

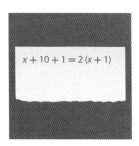

equation
[ĭ kwā/zhən]

area of path = 24 sq. ft.
area of brick = 2 sq. ft.
24/2 = 12 bricks

geometry
[jē äm/ə trē]

hospital
[häs/pĭ tl]

painter
[pān/tər]

pickup truck
[pĭk/ŭp trŭk/]

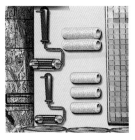

rollers
[rō/lərz]

tape measure
[tāp/mĕzh/ər]